EMERGENCE

REVEAL YOUR ESSENCE

8/5/19

Tamara;
Thank you for being part of this process!
The physical place of where this was processed
so grateful! Best to you! Fran and Matt

FRAN BAILEY

PHOTO AND ILLUSTRATION CREDITS

Photo page 19 & 72 © Dan Bailey, illustration on page 36 © Karolina Szymkiewicz, illustration on page 55 © Bruce Harman, photo page 104 © Helen Adams

Yongkang Dan / Shutterstock.com
sokolova_sv / Shutterstock.com
Amir Azeri / Shutterstock.com
Anneka / Shutterstock.com
Subbotina Anna / Shutterstock.com
Olaf Holland / Shutterstock.com
YJ.K / Shutterstock.com
Billion Photos / Shutterstock.com
JBCorl / Shutterstock.com
Sergey Nivens / Shutterstock.com

© Copyright 2019 Fran Bailey

Library of Congress INFO TK
Borrum et, que ni rem digendae nihite elit es rem nullab illecae-pro cone simodi nonet quidi tem eribus et ipsam eatus et dolore, quaectet aut hillaborem ea ant est, alitem inum et volest lab ilibera-tur, consequae voluptus molo quid quia doluptus.

1 2 3 4 5 6 7 8 9 10

EDITOR: Jessica Bryan
EDITORIAL ASSISTANT: Matthew Schweppe
PROOFREADER: Karen Schrier
COVER AND INTERIOR DESIGN: Karla Baker

All rights reserved. No part of this book may be used or reproduced by any means, graphic, electronic, or mechanical, including photo-copying, recording, taping or by any information storage retrieval system without the written permission of the author except in the case of brief quotations embodied in critical articles and reviews.

Balboa Press books may be ordered through booksellers or by contacting:

Balboa Press
A Division of Hay House
1663 Liberty Drive
Bloomington, IN 47403
www.balboapress.com
1 (877) 407-4847

Because of the dynamic nature of the Internet, any web addresses or links contained in this book may have changed since publication and may no longer be valid. The views expressed in this work are solely those of the author and do not necessarily reflect the views of the publisher, and the publisher hereby disclaims any responsibil-ity for them.

ISBN: 978-1-9822-2402-8 (sc)
ISBN: 978-1-9822-2401-1 (e)

Library of Congress Control Number: 2019903432

Print information available on the last page.

Balboa Press rev. date: 04/03/2019

*Love is forever present—
it is divine energy that keeps
us awake and connected.*

The process of life on earth
is the creation of love.

The real character lives inside you
and holds you dearly.

Allow love to be present.
It is your right to know love,
feel love, and embrace love.

DEDICATION

I dedicate this book to my loving handsome husband, Dan, who kept me laughing as he waited patiently for me to finish this book. To my children, who have taught me more than they can even imagine, Peter, Mary, and Charlie.

To my parents, who individually and together have taught me about love and all of its dimensions! I am so grateful for you both. Jane and Whit, bless you for creating a tradition in faith and love. To my sisters, Jenny and Muff, who continue to emulate this tradition in their own way as we bond to manifest it in our own families.

To my extended family Daniel H. Bailey, Amy Sebby, Heath, Sabina, Fiona, and Sadie MacKay.

To my dedicated students and clients, who continue to stay on the conscious path! Love! Love! Love!

NOTE FROM THE AUTHOR

Emergence is an invitation to experience thought as energy and how it affects your heart, mind, body, and spirit. We all experience a transference of energy every day with the people with whom we communicate, work, and live. If you think about how much is said without words it is amazing! The natural phenomenon of the New Moon Solar Eclipse in 2017 was a major shift of energy that was felt all over the world. What was experienced? The essence of stillness, the natural creative process of change in shadow and light, and the human connection as we all experienced something bigger than us. Emergence offers an opportunity to engage in stillness and consciously connect to the language of your own energy. You may be surprised as you witness and embrace your own creative process in another light. Beauty is what we see, feel, hear, and know in every sacred experience. Enjoy!

PRAISE FOR EMERGENCE

The first time I met Fran, sometime in the late '90s, she paused in the middle of our conversation and placed her hand on the center of my chest. While she held it there, I remember feeling a sense of calm, followed by the thought, "Hmm, there is something about this woman who is about to forever change my view of the world." At the time I had no idea what that even meant. The concepts in this book are simple, but don't be fooled, fully understanding them from within is a lifelong journey. Let Fran be your guide. You'll be glad you did.

Tom D'Erminio, LISW, and co-founder of The Affinity Center, Cincinnati, Ohio

Love, acceptance, letting go . . . the essences of what it means to be human. Yet, the misalignment of these concepts leads to endless human suffering. Fran Bailey, through her passionate SHEVA approach, adeptly teaches us how to begin to re-align our energies, cultivate our creativity and believe in our intuition. Particularly relevant today, this enlightening book is a must read.

John Sacco, MD, core faculty at University of Cincinnati Center for Integrative Health and Wellness, Cincinnati, Ohio

In *Emergence*, Fran shares her in-depth knowledge about the connection between the spiritual and corporeal realm and how we can communicate between the two effectively to reach a higher level of consciousness through the ancient chakra system. While much has been written and studied about the chakra system, Fran has a fresh approach for the reader to access and utilize internal knowledge to understand the intuition we all have to help us grow and expand to our full potential. As someone who has studied the chakra system, I found this book to be very enlightening and surprisingly simple as to its effectiveness. Anyone who is looking for a deeper understanding of themselves will find *Emergence* appealing and approachable.

Itaal Shur, Grammy Award-winning composer and musician

CONTENTS

ACKNOWLEDGMENTS 12

FOREWORD 13

EMERGENCE THROUGH THE SHEVA METHOD 15

PREFACE 20

ENERGY CENTERS

FIRST CHAKRA
TO FEEL SAFE 29

SECOND CHAKRA
TO CREATE 37

THIRD CHAKRA
TO RELEASE FIXATIONS 45

FOURTH CHAKRA
TO ACCEPT AND RECEIVE 53

FIFTH CHAKRA
TO CLEARLY COMMUNICATE 63

SIXTH CHAKRA
TO INTEGRATE 73

SEVENTH CHAKRA
TO KNOW 83

INNERLINK MEDITATION 93
   ACTIVATING YOUR ENERGY 94
   STIMULATING YOUR ENERGY 96
   REGENERATING YOUR ENERGY 98

IN CONCLUSION 101

RESOURCES 102

ABOUT THE AUTHOR 104

ACKNOWLEDGMENTS

I am truly grateful to be able to share my gifts and skills with those who have allowed me to guide them into the unknown with trust and vulnerability as they move toward new discoveries and identities. I thank my many teachers, students, clients, family, and friends for believing in this path of consciousness and in me.

During my years of teaching, I have had the luxury of focusing on small-group classes to effect real shifts and changes in the everyday lives of my students. Their commitment and support of each other creates a level of trust that results in a strong format for group and individual change. They continue to teach me as we stay on the path of consciousness. Bless you all.

Matt, Matt, Matt! What can I say? You are truly a gift and I am forever grateful for the question you have been asking me for the past year: "What do you mean, Fran?" I could not have done this without your clarity, expert computer skills, and analogies! With great admiration and love. Thank you.

Gloria, my teacher, friend, and colleague—what an incredible teacher and healer you are. I am glad we crossed paths. My love for you stretches out into all dimensions. Also, I want to thank you and John for recognizing the old soul in me and reminding me that I am as "old as dirt."

Thanks also to:

The Affinity Center in Cincinnati, Ohio, for the years of support.

The Conscious Living Center in Cincinnati, Ohio, for their community support and study of the Enneagram.

Steve Murphy and the team at Steve T. Murphy Law LLC for legal support and guidance.

Dr. Suzy Kramer for analyzing body movement and validating which meridians and acupressure points are used.

Erin Elizabeth Wells, M.DIV, for business consultation.

Sharon Finch for the timely astrological guidance from decades of experience.

Jane E. Simon for your foresight and encouragement.

Julie, Brian, Tom, Connie, Allison, and Margaret — Thanks for graciously sharing your stories.

EMERGENCE THROUGH THE SHEVA METHOD

We all struggle in life in one way or another at times. How we process our experiences decides whether we recover our balance, or not. If you choose to walk a conscious path, suffering can be circumvented through awareness of habits and patterns. By honoring our experience, we can flow and grow with life rather than being in resistance to it. When facing a challenge, do you resist or embrace the opportunity?

Human beings undergo many processes—just as in nature, there is a beginning, a middle, and an end. Awareness of these cycles can aid in establishing a foundation for discovering a natural balance between the physical, mental, emotional, and spiritual aspects, through order and chaos. By honoring these cycles, we can emerge from these experiences more connected, aware, and conscious of ourselves.

We must remember what is real and that we are in charge of our destiny. By accepting technology, our desire for instant gratification has become prominent. Trying to adapt to technological speed and constant interruption has impeded our desire to be connected to each other, the world around us, and with ourselves. Technology can help us achieve connection, but at the same time it can be persuasive, overwhelming, and addictive, with the potential to disconnect us from our essence. It's important for us as humans to stay connected to the messages from nature, Source, and one another in order to expand our consciousness and stay awake. As we multi-task in everyday life, it's important to include the multi-intelligences of the mind, heart, body, and soul for our essence to emerge. Tapping into the multidimensional self helps enrich everyday life and keeps the intrigue alive as we experience the mystery, magic, and miracles of life.

A METHOD FOR CONNECTION

The SHEVA Method of Emergence and finding your own essence is primarily about grounding and connecting with your own authentic energy. We are in constant collaboration with others and participate in situations that require us to be consciously present. Developing tools to stay awake and centered creates more balance and structure for a strong foundation. For example, letting go of what we think must be, ought to be, or have to be is often called "letting go of perfect pictures." Holding on to our desire for a perfect outcome in

Rest in exploration, creation and love.

any situation can be disappointing when it does not turn out the way we wanted. Identifying this as a repeated pattern—or energetic loop of constant disappointment—can affect the body and cause the collapse of the third chakra. Letting go of the desire for a perfect outcome is a great tool in finding our authentic energy.

Finding our essence means merging with the authentic self. It requires us to let go of the habitual patterns (or fixations) that keep us in resistance. Certainly, life has its obvious responsibilities, which cannot be avoided, but the concept of finding our own boundaries, patterns, and what affects us helps define our energy consciously. It keeps us awake to the traps we sometimes put ourselves in. We all have behaviors and anxieties that keep us in resistance to enjoying life as it is. This work is about the probability of change for those who desire to connect to the essence of physical, emotional, and spiritual collaboration. This process provides a creative and deeper understanding of emerging self-love and compassion for others.

As an example of emergence, one of my long-time clients had a herniated disc[1] and was told by his primary care physician that he needed to see a surgeon and get an MRI immediately or he might never walk again.

When he came to me for energy work, he was already scheduled for surgery but was open to the idea of resolving his herniated disc with an alternative approach. During our session, deeper underlying issues were revealed about the pain he was carrying and he allowed the energy to move by addressing the emotional impact and suffering. In doing so, the hernia disintegrated naturally, which made surgery unnecessary. We will dive deeper

---

[1] "Herniated disc" refers to damage in one or more of the rubbery cushions (discs) between the individual vertebrae (bones) that make up the spine.

into the details of this remarkable story and others in the second section of this book when we look at embodying this work.

SHEVA is a self-healing process that requires you to be present to the collaboration between your body, heart, mind, and soul.

Wherever you are in your journey, remember that all experience is sacred. Everything that comes up for you is valid, whether you perceive it to be right or wrong. Learning to trust what might be missing, disconnected, or resisted can guide you in understanding yourself more intimately, while experiencing life as it is.

If you choose to take your journey further, begin to play with the idea of curiosity, creativity, vulnerability, and accountability as ingredients for change. SHEVA acknowledges the basic human desires to feel safe, to create, to let go, to love, to communicate clearly, to integrate, and to know that we are all one.

It's important to have a sense of innocence, faith, humor, and courage when we are looking to embody the desires of the heart.

The core of this work is awareness of our own energy to support change. When we are energetically misaligned, the body is likely to show us through pain. The mind might chatter incessantly and the spirit might feel disconnected. It is no mistake that *endocrinology*—the study of how stress, emotions, and trauma affect our bodies—is prevalent. As you learn to embrace your own energetic awareness, it will become an intimate communicator for your health and well-being. Self-discovery begins with bridging the gap between self-doubt and self-certainty through grounding, acceptance, and love! By putting this energy into action, you can create a strong foundation to manifest your soul purpose in everyday life.

As one SHEVA participant remarked: "Wow—how we neglect ourselves. Sometimes we realize it only when we decide to take a workshop that someone has suggested."

This work allows us to have a new and deeper understanding of each other and ourselves.

By moving through resistance, we can experience positive energy and emotional relief. We experience *lightness* from letting go of our old, stuck energy. When we experience our own positive energy, we reconnect with links to the past and forge pathways to a future in which there is an undeniable connection to the *here and now*.

It's a natural direction to grow from this work and experience mystery, beauty, discovery, and elation. Through understanding our own energy and embracing our gifts it is possible to heal by establishing personal boundaries and finding the authentic self.

A therapist called me and said that she had ignored the signs for too long and needed to understand what she was experiencing.

So I said, "What are you experiencing?"

"I can't really explain it," she replied, "but I just *know* things and I am beginning to trust it more. I guess I need validation that I am on the right track. I want to investigate this further and utilize it in my life."

During our subsequent session, it was revealed that she no longer wanted to resist her intuitive abilities. As I observed her energy, I noticed that self-doubt was interfering with her ability to *know*, so I encouraged her to believe in her intuition and use it as a tool to integrate and trust. Only through acceptance could she embrace her gifts.

If you desire change,
but you are not quite sure
how it will manifest,
trust in the process.

suggestion for presence

Take a moment to be still while holding this book between your hands. With your eyes closed, imagine the energy flowing between them for at least twelve seconds. This will enable you to focus and experience the present moment.

When you are ready, open your eyes and then open the book to any random page. Notice where your attention is drawn and let yourself be in the experience and ready to emerge.

Let trust be your guide in this exploration, as you uncover the mystery in discovering your true purpose and how you fit into the bigger picture of your society and the world.

PREFACE

Can we maintain a sense of awe as we experience the mystery of life and its challenges, while facing the good, the bad, and the ugly?

Being in a state of wonder is the impetus for where this work begins. With wonder as a stimulus and foundation for discovery, we can have a deeper understanding of our experiences in the flow of life.

Sometimes our experiences in life are difficult to explain, and this becomes increasingly the case as our inquisitiveness draws us toward understanding profound questions, such as why we exist. If we are willing to embrace the mysterious, we can experience the miraculous.

My driving force and curiosity in combining true art, science, and human connection as part of the equation for healing became the foundation and expression of The SHEVA Method. Fortunately, motivated by my own exploration in healing, I was led to study with some amazing teachers and healers with many different backgrounds, including dance, philosophy, psychology, psychic and

"The most beautiful experience we can have is the mysterious. It is the fundamental emotion that stands at the cradle of true art and true science."

—*The World as I See It*, Albert Einstein

clairvoyant energy healing, acupuncture, and the enneagram.

These diverse expressions of art and science stimulated my deep passion and interest in healing through the mind, body, and spirit. Ultimately, I began contemplating the important questions: "Why are we here?" "How can I live a better life?" and "How can I make a contribution?"

The basic format and underlying concept this book revolves around is the notion that everything is energy and everything is connected. The famous drawing of the Vitruvian Man by Leonardo da Vinci represents the unification of art and science. It offers us the opportunity to experience probable proof that incredible beauty and mystery are the structure of human existence.

Art can be a stimulus to experience the mystery of life, whether it is a drawing or a sculpture that makes you contemplate with wonder an artist's incredible talent, a dancer's moves synchronized with the music in perfect form, or music that makes you cry. When you climb a mountain to the top to photograph the vastness of space, or when you view the fall colors and sit still in silence for a moment to soak in the surrounding beauty of nature, what do you experience? Perhaps it is a feeling, a sense of knowing, a sense that you are a part of universal truth!

To be able to play in this experiment of life, while trusting the process of unfolding in the ultimate truth of love, brings forth a sense of encouragement and faith that embodies all of your present experience.

At the age of three, I started dancing and was barely able to reach the barre, but when I heard the music resonate through me, I had the sensation of being at home, in a natural state of being. My reality was transformed into a state of bliss. From that moment forward, I wondered how people could arrive at such a place?

Early one morning when I was six years old, I was kneeling in front of a round coffee table holding a globe, singing: "I've got the whole world in my hands . . ." There are no words to adequately describe what happened next. I saw and felt myself as part of the universal connection. Little did I know what the connection would be, or that it would be reinforced throughout my life and validate the work ahead.

At home, I was brought up with metaphysical principles and ideas. It is ingrained in me that through our thoughts and interaction with the energy of God or the Source, or whatever you choose to call it, we can change and improve our health and sense of well-being.

While studying dance in high school and college, my fascination with scientific and spiritual collaboration developed through reading Eastern and Western scientists and philosophers. I continued to have the desire to reach an audience through the expression of movement, although I still felt there was something missing. Unsure exactly what it was,

I continued pursuing how to reach the audience on a more spiritual level.

After marriage and having children—while teaching a dance class at a private school—one of the parents, Dr. Steve Amoils, an alternative practitioner, suggested that I had a gift of recognizing energy. His suggestion led me to study with Rosalyn Bruyere, a hands-on clairvoyant healer and author of *Wheels of Light*. These studies connected me back to that original feeling of knowing and universal connection I had experienced as a young child.

Moving forward in my own exploration of energy, I realized I could transfer energy from my feet to my hands. I discovered pure joy while being present to the healing needs of my clients. With this skill, I began to understand what energy transference means at a deeper level. The power of healing and dancing—dancing and healing—became a fulfilling passion of expression, even as I feared but welcomed the unknown.

Then life brought me to my knees, as I faced the challenges of my father dying, a brush with cancer, and nearly drowning. I had no other choice than to submit to life as it was. Only through acceptance would I be able to move out of resistance and explore untapped parts of myself. In doing so, I began to understand the human condition and myself more intimately. Deep chakra meditation with clairvoyant healers Gloria Hemsher and John Friedlander helped me develop my own psychic abilities (see the Resources section). With this awareness of energy, I discovered ways to more efficiently heal others and myself.

It was my intention to create a preventative and restorative system others could learn that could be used to heal all aspects of themselves through a deeper conscious awareness and alliance of body, heart, and soul. In 2002, the phrase "Seeking Harmony in Energy, Voice, and Action" (SHEVA) was channeled to me for use in my healing practice. Little did I know at the time that it would slowly become the foundation for a method I would create, teach, and live by.

Countless hours were spent in my studio being present to my body, honoring the fact that the body would reveal the truth and return to health and wellness if I was willing to submit and listen. Whether it was a sharp pain, a sore muscle, or some other sensation, I saw these signs and symptoms as the body indicating there was an impediment to the natural flow of energy. Through addressing these issues and *feeling the release*, harmony of the mind, body, and spirit was not only possible, it was a natural state.

With my body as a guide for experiencing the energy flow through many cycles of self-observation, a technique emerged that utilized the inherent systems within the body. Anyone can use this technique to restore optimal functioning. In part, this includes a unique combination of movement that utilizes the acupressure points, chakra centers, and

Dancing intimately with the body/soul/mind experience touches the authentic relationship between you and the world.

meridian systems to move energy through the body and remove clutter from the mind.

Throughout my years of experience of body awareness as a dancer and energy healer, plus intense study in meditation and chakra clearing, I noticed that the assimilation of all these skills could provide clarity, distinction, and balance.

As I continued to explore resistance and flow of energy, I developed a fascination with personality fixations and how energy can get stuck by our own stubbornness and feeling we are right. I enrolled in an Enneagram class, which is a study of personalities originally designed by George Gurdjieff, a Russian teacher of esoteric knowledge in the 1930s. It has gone through many stages of development, but basically it is a study of nine different personality types. "Ennea" means "nine," which represents the number of points on a geometric figure called the *enneagram*. During this process, I had to look at my own resistance and fixations, which revealed many of my insecurities. Surprise, surprise . . . In essence, we are all types, although we tend to fixate on one

"Fran uses acupressure points and chakra centers, movement and gesture, and posture and focus with the ultimate effect of enhancing function and enhancing awareness of self."

— Dr. Susy Kramer, medical acupuncturist

more than the others. (See the Resources section in the back of this book for more information.)

As I became a facilitator of the enneagram, I learned more about the human condition and how we function. This, in turn, helped me clarify the whys and why nots of resistance and flow—and learn to accept the good, the bad, and the ugly in all of us. Combining knowledge of the Enneagram with body awareness and meditation skills, The SHEVA Method started to take form. This discovery has been consistently enlightening, and it continues to awaken me more with each new experience. The ride can be a bit bumpy at times, but there is joy in the journey. And that joy is experiencing the true self.

ENERGY CENTERS

The universe is made up of energy, just as our bodies are. According to Hindu beliefs, all living things carry the life force. The Hindus call these life force centers *chakras*, a Sanskrit word that means *wheels*. These energy centers are 360 degrees in diameter and run along the spine from the tailbone to the top of the head. There are seven chakras, each with a different meaning and frequency in the body. All of the information we receive passes through these energy centers, and all physical, mental, emotional, and spiritual intelligences respond accordingly.

To better identify where these centers are located, imagine energy flowing inside the body along the spine and collected in seven spheres. Each has a different feeling and purpose that can reveal information.

Please try something for me. If you are sitting, place your fingertips gently together in a triangle shape. When you notice the energy running through your fingertips, hold it for ten seconds. Now notice the vibrating energy inside your hands! Fantastic? Yes! Each energy center has a different frequency that can be experienced, and the exercises in this book are intended to provide an understanding of the energetic system and how to move energy throughout your body with greater awareness.

Each chakra has a different density, frequency, function, and focus. In the next several pages, we will discuss the meaning of each chakra and how we can keep them in balance.

The first and second chakras are always connected to and supported by earth energy. Please be aware that if you decide to do this meditation, there is no right or wrong. It's all about the experience and what you observe. Each person has things to address at different times. The body doesn't lie. If there is a specific energy center that is blocked, this kind of study and awareness will show you where you need to unblock.

For example, if you had a recent trauma, your first chakra might be difficult to connect to because you are in a fragile state. However, this is the perfect time to learn to stay centered. Throughout these experiential exercises, you will be given tools to clear and balance the thoughts and energies in each chakra. You will learn how to break down the barriers that create disconnection and separation. Developing this practice is the key to creating new energy for yourself and letting go of nagging thoughts, persistent pictures, and repeated patterns.

All information passes through all chakras at all times. Whatever you notice is a clue telling you the direction to be taken for healing. You might notice a block, less flow, detachment, or disconnection. Looking at what arises is part of the process of chakra alignment to connect your body, mind, and spirit. Understanding your own energy and how you process it will add another dimension of self-communication. Each of the following chapters includes a specific exercise intended to target the corresponding energy center.

SHEVA

SEEKING

HARMONY

in **E**NERGY

VOICE

& **A**CTION

A simple approach for enriching everyday experience and embodying who you truly are through awareness of your own energy.

FIRST CHAKRA

TO FEEL SAFE
safety / survival

First and foremost to create a safe space
where you can rest and focus.

What does feeling safe mean to you? We all have incredible instincts, and learning to discover and trust our primal instincts connects us to nature and the basic foundation of survival. Using Mother Nature as our model for understanding the ebb and flow, cycling and recycling, and order and chaos can assist us in knowing the underlying flow of life. We return to balance and safety as we are tested.

The picture of an elephant holding a baby in her trunk illustrates the feeling of complete safety. It reminds us of our connection to nature as part of the mystery and beauty of the universal truth that we all want to feel safe, accepted, and loved.

Think back to the first time you felt your survival was threatened. What did you do? Where did you go to feel safe? What did your inner voice tell you? Do your fear and anxiety draw you away from feeling safe?

Do fearful thoughts come directly from our imagination or indirectly from media, friends, or politics? Call on your instincts and focus on letting go of the "what ifs" in order to overcome your doubts and fears, and return to balance and feeling secure. Trust your instinct that you have the power to overcome fear through the intelligences of your mind, heart, and body.

Balancing the first chakra with the earth through a root, or grounding cord, is vital to support your journey. As we continue to move through the chakra system, the grounding cord will remain as a strong foundation. We all get rattled in life. When you get pulled off track, this simple reminder will assist you in reconnecting.

We all have experiences that provide us with the ingredients to survive. Do you call on your basic instinct and knowing? In your first experience of survival did you go into fight or flight? What brings you back to feelings of safety and how do you create it?

"Resistance to letting go and opening up to more space and freedom came with the encouragement of others. Awareness of the energy field behind me was under the radar, and the possibility of being able to fulfill my entire aura without the fear of being hurt. The thought arose of: What would happen if I let this go? Concerned with being present to all of me, there was the surrender of allowing the paradox and duality of both, and knowing that I was capable of handling a situation in which I was able to feel safe within myself and okay with the unknown, while not clinging to the past hurt."

— Matt Schweppe

trigger point location to activate the first chakra

The best way to locate the first chakra is to place your thumbs on top of your hip flexors (located where the hips and legs meet) and wrap your hands around your hips. Be sure to press your thumbs down toward the sit bones.

let go . . .

of any insecurity and
trust the process as you
move up the body
to the next energy center,
the creative center,
the second chakra.

SECOND CHAKRA

TO CREATE
expression

To experience the flow and movement of emotions
through order and chaos with an ability
to express yourself freely.

The second chakra is all about the freedom to create without fear or boundaries. This is a lovely place to be and share with others. Feeling grounded and supported, you can dance, sing, play loud music, write, draw, and totally immerse yourself in a state of flow. Clearing the second chakra creates passion and purpose.

Feeling safe and balanced provides the canvas for us to be able to create without fear. Being without fear allows us to remember our innocence and our imagination to flourish. This stimulating energy in the second chakra inspires us to let go, listen, feel, and trust our creative expression. Part of owning our creative center involves saying hello to our passion, purpose, and primal instincts in order to develop what we truly want.

Just as an artist creates and recreates again and again to find his or her freedom of expression, we also do this when we are not sure of our boundaries. For example, when we allow our mother's "shoulds," society's "have tos," religion's "ought tos," or "must be perfect pictures" to control us, our freedom to create can be pushed aside. Part of the process in finding your own creativity is discerning and defining your boundaries and letting go of responsibilities that are not yours. Tapping into the power of your emotions, sexual instinct, and boundaries is part of the design to express your creative skills and feelings. The creative place lies innocently within us without judgment or anticipation. Let yourself breathe . . .

As a modern dancer my artistic tool was my body, the stage was my canvas, and music was my impetus and stimulus to express how I viewed life. "Particles" was a piece with three dancers swirling like Sufi dancers lost in the moment of the music and movement. This artistic expression intended for the audience to feel the energy and be a part of the experience. If you are passionate about something and want to express it, let go of the "should nots" and get out of your own way to allow the creativity to flow. Feel the energy, the pulse of creation, and enjoy the experience as you allow it to synchronize in your everyday life. Interestingly, when you feel safe you can create, and in the process of creation your freedom and safety can be affirmed.

> "I am enough of an artist to draw freely upon my imagination. Imagination is more important than knowledge. Knowledge is limited. Imagination encircles the world."
>
> — Albert Einstein

Strength, Courage, and Wisdom, a song by the musical artist India Arie, includes these lyrics that appropriately describe how we can get to a place of inner knowing. She describes putting her fear aside and listening to her inner voice:

Behind my pride there lives a me that knows humility
Inside my voice there is a soul, and in my soul there is a voice
But I've been too afraid to make a choice
Cause I'm scared of the things that I might be missing
I've gotta step out on faith; it's time to show my faith
Procrastination had me down but look what I have found, I found
Strength, courage, and wisdom
And it's been inside of me all along . . .
Behind my pride there lives a me that knows humility
Inside my voice there is a soul, and in my soul there is a voice
But I've been too afraid to make a choice
Cause I'm scared of the things that I might be missing
I've gotta step out on faith; it's time to show my faith
Procrastination had me down but look what I have found, I found
Strength, courage, and wisdom
And it's been inside of me all along . . .

trigger point location to activate the second chakra

The second chakra is located from the pubic bone to the belly button. To make contact, place your right hand in front and your left hand in the back of the second chakra, where the sacrum is located, and feel the energy between your hands. Remember, the chakras are 360 degrees. Press your right hand toward the center of your body and your left hand toward the center of your body, and imagine the energy meeting in the middle.

let go . . .

of any guilt or shame
that stops you from
being your most creative self,
*as you move up to the third chakra
and empower your creative ideas.*

THIRD CHAKRA

TO RELEASE FIXATIONS
empowerment

Using energy authentically to
embrace a balanced ego.

We all have conflict and traumas in our lives that test us one way or another. The point is in how we handle it! By coming back to our truth and basic foundation, a balanced life will return and create a flow of energy as we embrace each experience. Consciously developing our awareness of how we process and integrate the physical, emotional, and spiritual body is key to having less resistance.

As we deal with the third chakra, we constantly cycle through a process of creation, destruction, and recreation in order to develop a healthy ego and submit to the basic foundation of love.

Sometimes life brings us unexpected events and challenges that directly affect our ego. Do we take these moments as lessons to learn from and discover our authentic power, or do we remain in a fixated pattern? How we are being judged, or how we are judging ourselves, is the platform from which the ego jumps. If we are willing to be present to our reactions in challenging situations, we can develop a healthy ego and a natural and confident sense of self. We will exist without judgment.

Through this work you can begin to see the patterns you cling to. It's okay to be confused. It's how we learn to let go and move beyond the story—away from our fixated state and into neutrality and authenticity.

When we are ungrounded and react from a state of confusion, does our ego retreat or dominate? When we are grounded and conscious, healthy empowerment unfolds naturally.

JULIE'S EXPERIENCE

Julie was recovering from breast cancer when she came to see me. She was in the process of reevaluating her life and what mattered.

"I have been working on this project for weeks with the motivation to simplify and throw out unnecessary 'stuff,' she said. "But yesterday it hit me—I am trying to remember who I am, what I love, and what is whole and beautiful in my life. I want to remember (or figure out) how I want to live, and throw out the unnecessary stuff inside of me—not just the items in the closet."

As George Eliot said, "It's never too late to be what you might have been."

Whether you are struggling with a life crisis or finally deciding to make a long-desired change, releasing the fixations can empower the shift. Letting go of the "shoulds," "have tos," and "oughts" will allow you to hear your inner voice. You can't avoid life events; the challenge is in how you process the experience. Developing a healthy ego requires awareness of who you *are* and who you *are not*. Keeping this concept in mind as you meditate will eventually become a way of life and practice that supports a greater state of happiness.

This distinction allowed Brian to become reacquainted with his own energy and make the desired shifts to change his outlook. "I feel much better having removed some of that old energy that was holding onto me so tight. There is a lightness about it," he said. "You [Fran] are accelerating my awakening to my energy awareness and future capabilities."

Be confused; it's where you begin to learn new things. Be broken; it's where you begin to heal. Be frustrated; it's where you start to make more authentic decisions. Be sad, because if we are brave enough we can hear our heart's wisdom through it.
Be whatever you are right now.
No more hiding.
You are worthy, always.

— S.C. Lourie

trigger point location to activate the third chakra

Moving higher to the third chakra—located from the belly button to the diaphragm—place your right hand a little above your belly button and your left hand a little below the diaphragm. Hold for ten seconds as you breathe deeply.

let go . . .

of looking for answers outside of yourself, and pay attention to your shortcomings. *Allow love to show up in the fourth chakra!*

FOURTH CHAKRA

TO ACCEPT & RECEIVE
to love and be loved

To contact and live in the heart center,
the source of love. It is the place where we
feel all is right in the world . . . and with us in it!

The direction and momentum in the heart chakra is to move toward accepting our imperfections and learn to love unconditionally without judgment. This can be hard at times, but love stands at the altar of truth. How you arrive at discovering your own truth is your own process and choice.

Through the third chakra, we address the barriers of the ego that have created resistance against love. In the fourth, we are looking to empower all shades of love from self, relationships, and the divine.

When have you felt love? Was it while holding your father's hand or experiencing your mother's embrace? Have you been moved by the love of a pet or the beauty of nature? Have you felt love during moments of complete surrender, such as when laughing with your best friend or embracing your lover?

The confusion between need and love, and want and desire, arises when the barriers of the ego are not addressed. Ask yourself these simple questions to help reveal the barriers of your ego in relation to

Love—being at the altar of truth—provides an instinctual understanding of what is, without question. You can now ground, create, and be present in love as you continue the process of creating what you want in harmony!

self-love: What does love mean to me? Am I in a relationship of love or need?

Many of us have been in relationships where our needs are not being met or the person is not right for us. If we stay in a relationship that is not working, it will affect us one way or another through the mind, body, or heart. As discussed before, the body doesn't lie. Emotions and thoughts can get energetically trapped in and around the body, which can be expressed physically through pain. Each of us holds our pain in different places in our body.

LOVE IN RELATIONSHIPS

Coming back to the story mentioned earlier about the client who was having terrible back pain from a herniated disc, it seems he was inclined to hold his pain in his heart.

Previously, he had undergone quadruple bypass surgery. At the time he came to see me, he was going through a dramatic separation, plus dealing with his ill mother. While visiting her, his disc herniated as he was picking up lint (of all things), causing extreme pain.

Prior to our session, I sensed that his physical pain stemmed from emotional strain and the fact that he felt trapped. It's important to create space for transformation in order to heal. As a healer, I honored his current emotions and state of general health, while also holding the potential for him to be healthy. One day while I was driving, I visualized his disc and saw that it was not damaged, but whole and healthy. What transpired during our subsequent session was quite amazing.

He arrived very discouraged because he was scheduled to have surgery the next day. However, he was open to trusting the process in order to avoid it. He sat down and I started to run energy through his left foot and then to his shoulder. The pain got worse at first, like it was in his back. I asked him to keep letting go, and I simply suggested that he was not responsible for the pain of others. Immediately, he started to release energy and his tears began to flow. The accumulated effect of holding responsibility for others began to resolve slowly. I could feel the tremendous amount of heat coming off of him.

As I moved to his right knee, the intensity heightened and then the final attachment subsided as I continued to pull energy away from his body and energy field. My intuition and vision of the pain moving away from his body was physically manifested through collaboration that was free from judgment. Miracles are possible in such a space.

I asked him how he felt and he said the pain was gone from his back. He walked away without a limp.

I am not a medical doctor, so I suggested that he go back to the surgeon to check in and verify that everything was okay.

He went to see the doctor, who had cancelled his vacation to Hawaii to perform the surgery. The surgeon said, "Who are you working with and what do you do with this person?" My client replied, "Her name is Fran and we do stretching, meditation, and energy work. We also talk about emotions and energy."

From the lack of symptoms, the surgeon determined the operation wasn't necessary because the patient's hernia had resolved. He acknowledged that it was very rare for him to send patients out of his office without undergoing surgery. The doctor stated, "[Fran] already performed the surgery." Then he said, "Does she do anything with weight?"

After writing that last statement, the picture shown here came up on my computer without my touching anything. I believe there are no mistakes. This picture comes from a card I bought in Portland. It shows Quan Yin, Jesus, and Buddha as

> "Your task is not to seek for love, but merely to seek and find all the barriers within yourself that you have built against it."
>
> — Rumi

symbols of the waters of compassion and healing. First considered to be the "female Buddha," Quan Yin appeared in Chinese scriptures around 400 AD, her name meaning "one who hears the cries of the world." She has been part of my practice for many years. Compassion is a way of life and a way of viewing the world. Quan Yin is a spiritual gift that continues to appear when the need is there. So . . . I give you, Quan Yin, who said, "Keep your mind clear and your heart open so you can hear your truth."

SELF-LOVE

When our self-worth is questioned, we sometimes move into assumptions and the expectations of others. We impose demands because of our own insecurities. Our unmet needs can cause us to blame others for not loving us the way we want them to when, in fact, it could be our own self-loathing and perpetual thought of the fixated ego that causes our suffering. This is a perfect opportunity to meditate and look inside to see what is missing. Usually, if enough time is spent on self-love, rather than self-loathing, the problem will resolve itself and your expectations and needs will be met. Remember: thought is energy. Releasing unhealthy thoughts is part of the meditative process. The "story" of unworthiness you keep telling yourself will become less of a focus. It's a struggle sometimes to stay on a conscious path, but it's worth the effort to find the love inside of you.

UNIVERSAL LOVE

In order to love and be loved, we must create a level of vulnerability. Through recognition of the ego, we can let go and open the heart to experience compassion with the human condition. With this recognition, we will be capable of experiencing the oneness of humanity. When have you felt a universal connection? While this experience might differ for each person, it's important to know for yourself how and when this occurs. Experiencing this divine connection is part of the joy of being human.

LISTENING TO THE HEART'S INTELLIGENCE

Ever present love penetrates the heart/body, soul/spirit, and personality, feeding the conscious self, vitality, serenity, and peace.

Love gives life and vitality to everything we do. There is no limit or judgment in love.

Love opens the heart to what really matters.

Love makes no demands.

Love heals and assists in transcending negative thoughts in ourselves and others.

When we are out of resistance to love and we surrender to the light of love, the energy of love will permeate us and reflect out to those around us.

Love reflects love.

> "Divine love has met and will always meet every human need."
>
> — Mary Baker Eddy

trigger point location to activate the fourth chakra

The fourth chakra is located at the heart, centered in the chest. To make contact, place your knuckles together so your fingers are facing in toward your breastbone and press gently. Take a deep breath and allow the energy to flow into the heart chakra.

let go . . .

of the fear of rejection and
stay true to love of self,
with all its glory and shortcomings.
Get ready to say hello to the
multidimensional self,
as you move up to the fifth chakra.

FIFTH CHAKRA

TO CLEARLY COMMUNICATE
the authentic voice

To free the voice and speak from the heart.

As you move up to the fifth chakra, the energetic frequency becomes lighter and less dense. Keep in mind integrating the responses from each chakra: the instinct, the creator, the ego, and the heart's submission to the authentic voice in the fifth chakra. What does "authentic voice" mean?

The authentic voice comes from understanding your real concerns and needs in any given situation. Accessing what genuinely lies beneath the surface helps to address issues that work best for each person involved. When practiced, you may observe doubt, fear, control, or anger.

Some of us have an easy time expressing our thoughts; some of us don't. What happens when we doubt our own response or when we are not allowed to speak?

Do we feel inadequate in our word choices? Do we feel that we won't be heard or we will be dismissed? Perhaps we are boastful, demanding, or self-righteous. Part of this aligning process is to understand how all of our energetic centers are connected and integrated at all times. This can offer clues as to how and why we respond in a certain way. What kind of experiences did you have growing up? Did you have an over-bearing parent? Did a teacher test your self-worth? Did a classmate speak up more than you and become the teacher's pet? Perhaps you are an emotional person who feels so much it is hard to get the words out.

I grew up with two sisters. In our family, it was better to be seen and not heard. At the dinner table, my father would do most of the talking. He did not allow us to speak, and as a result we experienced a certain level of dismissal. This caused me to feel angry, but I didn't know how to handle it at the time. Dancing became my way of expression—and finding my voice through movement wasn't all bad. Times were changing very quickly in the '60s and rebellion against how things were done was rising. I am sympathetic toward my father now, what with all those women in the house. He changed with the times as best he could and eventually became a man of true love and wisdom.

Watching my father in his role as a husband, father, and provider, it was interesting to see how easily human beings can get caught in the roles we are expected to play. After his battle with addiction and almost losing his family, money and success weren't as important to him anymore. He rose above his addiction, and his family became his priority. He loved words and wrote poetry all the time as a form of authentic expression. Here is one of his poems:

SAND

King's horses, knights, a trumpet bank
wove paths along each grain of sand—
An empire in an endless list
Of empires cut of amethyst.

Great light woke dreams from outer black
in cadences of thunder crack.
Infinity began without an end
In rivers curving past a bend.

Man learns enough to hold a place—
for living in a living race—
The great experiment is born
In night along the early morn.

— Benjamin Whitney Lamson, Jr.

Communicating clearly while honoring and hearing each other fully might be the best ingredient for making decisions and taking action with complete authenticity. How wonderful it would be if we were conscious enough to make it happen all the time.

This is our goal. Yes! Watching my father change and respect himself and others around him by expressing his love and appreciation for life was a huge influence on me. I am truly grateful. Funny how it all works!

Right here where you and I stand, we shall behold a true and radiant world. In that world, we shall dance only our divine essence.

— Ruth St. Denis

When the fifth chakra is in balance, our words flow from the physical, emotional, and mental intelligence naturally.
Our thoughts thread together with ease via balanced collaboration with new avenues of creativity arising authentically from the heart.

FORGIVENESS

Imagine forgiveness as an impetus to freedom:

Forgive and free yourself from all the wrong you think you have done. Patiently wait, allowing this concept to arise and integrate within you; feel yourself letting go of all judgment.

When you are ready, release guilt, shame, blame, or doubt coming from you or others.

Bring attention to the inner voice. It can reveal the truth and set you free to unveil a deeper connection to the higher creative self. Experiment with the idea that divine energy is always beside you, waiting to be accepted.

Breathe . . .

Listen! Let go and live in love.

Treasure life's magical experience and witness all that is, while embracing the human connection in love and harmony.

trigger point location to activate the fifth chakra

The fifth chakra is located at the throat. To make contact, place your thumbs on your collarbone, press gently, and wrap your fingers around to the back of your neck. Imagine energy emanating from your fingers and permeating into your cervical spine.

let go . . .

of suppressing thoughts that keep you from communicating what comes from the heart *and invite your intuition from the sixth chakra to voice your true expression.*

SIXTH CHAKRA

TO INTEGRATE
connect mind, body and soul

To create an opportunity to integrate
all aspects of who you are and emerge
more whole from the experience!

The unfolding continues in the sixth chakra, giving you more space to explore physical, emotional, mental, and spiritual collaboration. This chakra provides an opening for the natural intuitive self to shine light on a deeper connection and accept what is meant to be. The dichotomy in the sixth chakra is that while it is the intellectual center, it is also the intuitive and soul connection center.

THE INTELLECTUAL CENTER

Mental chatter arises from our intellect, and it can persist from holding on to thoughts of doubt, fear, and rightness. The consciousness we are looking for is awareness of this energetic pull and recognition of how persistent negative thinking can affect the body. Does the mind control the body, or does the body control the mind? It's an age-old question. Both are valid, but the body never lies. When we are in a state of confusion, we might react with an emotional outburst of anger or feel hurt. Our mental state could be that of denial, or perhaps we are set in a pattern that keeps us disconnected.

You will have more control of your mental chatter as you learn and practice meditation, and begin to understand your own intuition and its cues. This is a goal! Don't beat yourself up when your mind refuses to shut off. We are not perfect, and laughing at ourselves is always a good remedy, as in: "Oh my God. There is that thought again! Could I maybe cut that thought in half?" Connie realized that she was suppressing her intuition by being attached to the drama of a situation and was unable to separate her energy. In meditation, she began asking pivotal questions like, "Whose energy is it? What am I attached to?" Through this process she began to understand her "self-imposed isolation" and how she was in resistance toward her authentic self. She said, "The truths were courageously realized with the support, acceptance in our group meditations, and nature's intuitive whispers." This allowed her to move beyond intellectualization and be in joy.

THE INTUITIVE CENTER

Truly amazing things can happen when you allow yourself to view the insights that arise from your intuition. For example, while you are meditating, through the sixth chakra you might see in your mind an object, an event, or a person, experience a memory, or relive a conversation that is still contained within your energy field. The information you receive through the sixth chakra can give you a totally different perspective.

The sixth chakra offers the opportunity to use your psychic/clairvoyant skills—the ability to see events clearly in your "mind's eye"—in order to view your personal life situations with more dimension and expansion.

Coordinating the essence of the physical, emotional, and mental aspects of yourself creates the opportunity to embrace the intuitive self without resistance. This collaboration connects these centers of intelligence and allows us to experience spiritual wisdom.

Allison was in a meditative state when she experienced, "vivid colors, grounding roots, and . . . a safe space that has been difficult for [her] to find." Learning to trust her intuition allowed her to move beyond doubt and embrace the unknown in order to relieve the "stuck energies" and victimization to find self love. During a crisis of almost losing her eight-and-a-half-year-old daughter to cancer and going through a divorce, she was tested. Through this work she learned how to experience safety in tumultuous times with grounding. She often noticed she was ungrounded when her feet began to hurt—she would take this as an opportunity to clear the chakras, ground, and be present to her instinct and intuition.

Ask yourself these questions while in meditation: What am I observing? How am I seeing myself in this memory? What am I noticing that I did not see before? If we get out of our own way, a whole new experience and viewpoint can occur that will help us assimilate new information in everyday life with our intellect, intuition, and soul.

THE SOUL CONNECTION CENTER

Aligning all the chakras to this point can give you a direct line of communication to your spirit/soul. Try to imagine your soul being your best friend who has great advice for you—if you choose to listen. With this attitude, trust and collaboration with the universe (and you in it) begin to make sense. The bigger picture helps us move away from resistance and allows us to let go of that pesky energy that holds us back from true connection and feelings of belonging.

What is your purpose in life and what does life look like with you in it doing what you were meant to do? You are allowed to be here with all your imperfections, and with your soul as your best supporter and guide. It's comforting to know that we are able to play and learn as part of life on earth and thus reveal the real character inside of ourselves.

Below is a practical example of using these meditation skills in a group situation to rebuild a business, while capturing the soul purpose of the group's mission statement.

The Affinity Center, located in Cincinnati, Ohio, consists of an integrative group of therapists who use alternative therapies to address the effects of ADD and ADHD in adults and children. In 2011, they hired me to help with a transition after one of their leaders passed away. I had worked with some of the therapists and they were willing to take an alternative route using meditation and energy healing to support the inevitable change. Allowing time and space for grieving determined how they would move forward. Slowly, through weekly meditation practice, a new purpose and mission began to arise.

After a meditation clearing, the group energy began to surface in a new way. They started to realize the importance of this work and how to integrate it in their professional and personal lives. Utilizing energy by aligning all the chakras allowed an authentic creative process to unfold. A visual tool from the sixth chakra was introduced that formulated a metaphor that could navigate the team forward. This vision was a wagon wheel, with the center being their mission and each spoke representing a therapist. This helped to realign the organization and establish momentum for the wheel to spin in the right direction at the right speed. This metaphor helped to intuitively integrate their collective energy around their core mission and establish a new foundation for success.

"Principles for the Development of a Complete Mind: Study the science of art. Study the art of science. Develop your senses— especially learn how to see. Realize that everything connects to everything else."

— Leonardo da Vinci

trigger point location to activate the sixth chakra

The sixth chakra is located at the center of the head. To make contact, place your thumbs at each temple and interlace your fingers along the center of your forehead. Direct the energy from your thumbs and fingertips toward the center of your head, meeting in the middle at the pineal gland. This exercise can help stop mental chatter.

let go . . .

of doubting your essence!
Say hello to your spiritual self as you
move to the seventh chakra
and connect to a deeper source—
*to a sense of wholeness
and your soul purpose.*

SEVENTH CHAKRA

TO KNOW
recognition of innate wisdom

Awakening your true creative wisdom
while tapping into sources to support
your highest creative potential.

The seventh chakra represents the possibility of accepting and experiencing the unknown by simultaneously embracing faith in all of its emerging aspects, from primal to mental, emotional, and your spiritual essence. The most intriguing aspect of this is the absence of personality, with its egotistical demands and resistance to knowing and not knowing. The ultimate truth lies within you, accepting life as it is with your sacred relationship to God/Source and the universal message.

Opening the door to your highest potential means letting go of fear of the unknown and embracing the divine inside of yourself. It can be scary to feel complete acceptance!

Part of divine self-discovery is being in the divine energy that each individual creates. Through discipline and willpower, the divine energy unfolds for all to see. Faith develops through self-trust and soul respect. As the world is changing, our identity is changing. To stay on the path we must trust without fear of the unknown.

DIRECT KNOWING

The dichotomy is found within the concept of knowing and unknowing. By embracing the unknown, we can experience a new place of knowing with complete acceptance of what is and how we create in a world without doubt. We are what we create. Letting go of what we think we know can be overwhelming. In the process of surrendering, we let go of what we have known, which is often our resistance to experiencing the unknown. The battle of resistance can keep us awake, or keep us asleep. If we choose to stay awake, the door to the unknown is open with acceptance even in the face of uncertainty. In doing this work, we create an internal bridge between the knowing and the unknowing in order to embrace both. In this way, the experience becomes richer, more powerful, and meaningful.

What we perceive to be real and authentic might be right in front of us, beside us, or inside of us! Holding on to doubt can cause us to misinterpret what we already know. How we attach ourselves to doubt can be part of our personality, causing us to put our personal mark on what has to be true, should be true, and ought to be true. As we investigate these multidimensional parts of ourselves, imagine we could release the grip of doubt and feel the quality of energy shift and change, and trust ourselves in the present moment! Being in the heart of direct knowing occurs only in experiencing the experience. This collective energy of experience is what we live and strive for as we embrace love, compassion, faith, and truth!

When you secure your mental, physical, emotional, and spiritual collaboration by clearing each chakra up to the seventh, you establish a strong foundation upon which your body can be a vessel for experiencing the divine within. Allowing this level of vulnerability creates the opportunity for

Believing in your highest creative potential—while feeling safe and supported—creates a foundation that will enable you to connect with Source and deepen your relationship with it. Connecting to the original cell of creation provides a knowing of all that is. It will also allow you to experience the divine within yourself.

a whole new magical experience to manifest from the mysterious. By connecting to your highest creative potential, you will be able to live in alignment with your divine purpose and universal connection.

You might experience déjà vu in this space, a feeling of familiar energy, a recognition of knowing that which is beyond words, a moment when all of your senses are awake and connected—and your body, mind, and spirit are in sync with your highest level of trust.

In my classes and private sessions, I call upon this highest level of trust to experience the energy through the help of my guides. Guides are supporters of your soul. They assist by nudging you through life to find your authentic purpose. These incorporeal/ethereal beings help us fulfill our spiritual contracts by encouraging us to pay attention to synchronicity, while honoring our intuition and gut.

Synchronicity in life is similar to when musicians improvise with their instruments to create a collective harmonized sound in each precious moment. My best performances as a dancer always included one musician. Together we would integrate music, movement, and energy spontaneously in the moment. The magic begins when you let go and allow the energy to come without imposing or resisting. Being free from fear allows you to be connected with the higher frequencies of your soul's essence. Your body becomes an aligned vessel to be one with divine energy—to begin accessing and channeling information.

I am grateful for receiving channeled messages and healings, which seem to always come at the right time. I have seen amazing shifts and changes in my clients and students. With practice and allowing the experience to unfold, wonderful things can happen. As one of my students, Margaret, explained: "During the most recent group meditation, after clearing the sixth and seventh chakras, I felt very calm and grounded. I was in a stress-free place, but then, in an instant I was distracted by a conversation with my ego and I needed to ground again to get out of the way so I could see, feel, and know. Then I saw the one I needed to see, and it was Jesus seated in meditation with pink on his heart, shining like a gem just for me. I was filled with love."

Some believe that Jesus studied with the Hindus during the fifteen years of his life not accounted for. In *Autobiography of a Yogi* by Paramahansa Yogananda, it is mentioned that Babaji taught Jesus about meditating for a deeper spiritual connection. Babaji is my main guide, and he has amazing spiritual and loving energy.

Babaji channeled the following to me while I was in meditation:

"The temple [the body] and the template [house] in which we live and create become more defined when the choice of a conscious path is taken."

"If those around you tend to be suffering from the desire for uncontrollable rightness, let it go. Try not to match the energy— it seems to waste precious time. Try to remember that life shows us differences for us to experience it all. Joy is in the experience. It works both ways. If we hold on to the perfect picture and demand the outcome, it confines the energy too much without a natural flow. As we strive to become awake and let go, we can rework ways to communicate."

— Babaji

This kind of channeled information is always informative, inspirational, and a reminder to stay awake and trust in the flow of the process. For the body, mind, and heart to create the changes you desire, imagine while meditating that every cell of your being is manifesting the collective energy of the experience so the healing and/or epiphany can adhere with grace, flow, and harmony.

Being courageous and embracing what arises will deepen and enrich your life. Each time an experience like this occurs, new levels of consciousness will emerge for you to integrate and embody—for you to live in alignment with your highest purpose. Being aware of what is happening in each moment allows us to process current energy and be present to the mystery, magic, and miracles of life. How lucky we are to play with what is most important to us.

trigger point location to activate the seventh chakra

To connect with the seventh chakra, place your fingertips on the top of your head and lightly connect to the energy of the seventh chakra across your skull.

let go . . .

of reason and unfold the possibilities!
Allow the body to guide you!
Accept the spirit to embrace you!

INNERLINK MEDITATION

TO ACTIVATE, STIMULATE & REGENERATE

clear and rejuvenate your chakras

A process to balance the energy centers
utilizing Earth and Cosmic Energy
to initiate the power of self-healing.

ACTIVATING YOUR ENERGY

Now that you have gained some intellectual knowledge about each chakra and its purpose, we are going to observe the energetic response as you move through these energy centers. We will begin to experience what energy is by observing what energy does. Remember, this is a study and observation practice. As you learn about your energy and how to utilize it more efficiently for support, try not to judge where you are *not*. As you learn and experience meditation clearing, certain emotions, thoughts, and awareness might light up for you, either immediately or you will recognize them later. Everything is timing, so trust in the experience and accept how the information speaks to you right when you need it and are ready to receive. This is not a test; there is no right or wrong pace—just your personal pace. The only requirement is to find the time, space, and presence in the moment to focus on meditation and learning.

TOOLS

In the following clearing exercise, visualized tools will be used so you can easily dissolve, release, and melt away anything that is not working for you.

For example, you might visualize putting the undesirable energy in a biodegradable bowl, or on a flower where you can let the petals drop. It's your choice!

You have the power
to be in charge of letting go
of what no longer serves you.

YOUR ENERGY FIELD

One important factor is to send the unwanted energy outside of your energy field, or aura. Everything has an energy field; for example, when you walk up to a tree you might sense, or feel, the strong energy around it. Try holding your arms straight out on each side of your body. This is how big your aura is. It also reaches above you, in front of you, and behind and below you. Visualize yourself as the yolk of an egg—the white of the egg is your energy field. The shell is the edge of your aura. This process of dissolving will be presented in each chakra as you clear energy that no longer works for you.

GROUNDING CORD

A grounding cord supports your first and second chakras. In the first chakra the grounding cord includes all of the female or male reproductive organs. Even if you don't have them, the energetic imprint still exists.

When you do this meditation, please also incorporate the left and right sciatic nerves, which are located on either side of the sacrum (the end of the spine). These nerves run down the back of the leg and attach to the heels.

In doing this clearing meditation, trusting and connecting to your body intelligence is key for you to remain grounded and connected.

COSMIC ENERGY

We will be using gold, cosmic energy, a lighter frequency, to assist and support in clearing the third through seventh chakras. Imagine it entering through the crown of the head and filtering down through the upper chakras.

STIMULATE YOUR ENERGY

Before you begin to clear your energy centers, find a comfortable and preferably quiet space that is conducive to meditation.

CREATE SPACE FOR A GROUNDING CORD

Imagine creating space at the base of your spine, and ask Mother Earth to connect to you with a grounding cord to support the trunk of your body, like a root. Get familiar with this feeling of rootedness to the earth. Sit and look around the room and see if you can call on the feeling of being safe. Let yourself breathe . . . feel your feet, your legs supporting your hips, and the energy moving in your spine. Feel the presence of your unique self, take a deep breath, and allow yourself to relax fully with the support of Mother Earth. Feel this soothing energy from the core of the earth, four thousand miles down. Utilize this grounding cord through the first and second chakras.

CLEARING THE FIRST CHAKRA

Bring your attention to the base of your spine where the grounding cord connects. Focus on your feet and repeat the phrase: "I trust my body to release any patterns and energy that do not serve me at this time." Then place the undesirable energy on the tool you have created using visualization. Continue clearing and repeating the phrase as you move up to your ankles, shins, calves, knees, thighs, and hip sockets. Placing this unwanted energy on the tools that you've created, send them out past the edge of your aura.

Moving into the base of your spine, you are about to clear the first chakra. Imagine a sphere in the center of your spine where you sit. As you create tools, remember the chakras are 360 degrees, so create tools in the front and back of your body, and on each side, to release energies that are not serving you. And now add the phrase: "I trust my body to release any energy and repeated patterns that are not serving me at this time." Allow the body to release any and all thoughts and feelings of insecurity and feeling unsafe in the first chakra.

CLEARING THE SECOND CHAKRA

Continue moving up your body to the second chakra (pubic bone to belly button), and ask your body to clear and release any fear of expressing your creative self in brilliant colors. Repeat the phrase: "I trust my body to release any energy and repeated patterns that are not serving me at this time." Remember to place this unwanted energy on the tools that you've created, sending them out past the edge of your aura.

CLEARING THE THIRD CHAKRA

Utilizing this gold, cosmic energy to assist, bring your attention to opening the third chakra (belly button to diaphragm) and begin again to clear any energies that are not serving you. Remember the chakras are 360 degrees. Create your tools and release any patterns that keep you fixated and stuck! Repeat this phrase while sending the energy out past your aura: "I trust my body to release any energy and repeated patterns that are not serving me at this time."

CLEARING THE FOURTH CHAKRA

Please notice that as we move higher to the fourth chakra at the heart, the frequency is lighter and less dense than it is in the lower chakras. As you begin to open up the fourth chakra and clear, include the shoulder socket, arms, and hands. Be aware of any feelings or sensations as you release and embrace the truth about what you want to create and open to the ultimate truth of love.

A reminder: Continue to check your grounding cord. This is very important because it will help you stay in your body as you move into these higher frequencies. Repeat this phrase: "I trust my body to release any energy and repeated patterns that are not serving me at this time."

CLEARING THE FIFTH CHAKRA

Now let's focus on the fifth chakra at the throat and release doubts related to your personal truth. Visualize and create tools to let any doubts go, and begin to say hello to your authentic voice and access your words of choice.

Now that you have come this far, it's time to start integrating and focusing on how this alignment can increase and support all aspects of self. Repeat this phrase: "I trust my body to release any energy and repeated patterns that are not serving me at this time."

CLEARING THE SIXTH CHAKRA

Now let's focus on the sixth chakra at the center of your head and let go of the excess chatter in your mind! Yes, that is right! Let it go! The physical, emotional, and mental aspects of self can now show up and collaborate! Repeat this phrase: "I trust my body to release any energy and repeated patterns that are not serving me at this time."

CLEARING THE SEVENTH CHAKRA

Now move to the top of your head and the seventh chakra in all its glory! Begin to let go of reason and allow your authentic purpose to unfold as you deepen your connection to Source. Believe in your highest creative potential, knowing the divine lives in you. Repeat this phrase: "I trust my body to release any energy and repeated patterns that are not serving me at this time."

REGENERATE YOUR ENERGY

Now that you have completed the clearing, there is one final and very important step:

Using your inner awareness, step outside of your body and scan yourself from top to bottom, letting go of any excess energy!

What is lingering might surprise you . . .

Put this energy on your tools and release it. Let it go down to the center of the earth, where Mother Earth will rejuvenate, regenerate, and recycle the energy you have given her.

Release your grounding cord but do not follow it!

Then create a new grounding cord! Have Mother Earth bring fresh new energy from the core of the earth, four thousand miles down, up to your first chakra, your reproductive organs, and your sciatic nerves. Feel the support and grounded feeling. Bring this new energy into your feet, ankles, shins, calves, knees, hip sockets, the first chakra base of the spine, and the second chakra (pubic bone to belly button). Regenerate!

From above the crown, bring fresh new cosmic energy into the seventh chakra at the top of the head, the sixth at the center of the head, the fifth at the throat, the fourth at the heart, and the third at the stomach. Regenerate!

Feel the connection and integration of earth and cosmic energy balancing your body and aura, or energy field.

Take a deep breath and thank your body for the work you have done. Say hello to the shifts and changes you have made. Congratulate yourself for a job well done!

WHAT YOU MIGHT HAVE OBSERVED DURING CLEARING

Someone else's energy in your space could be the result of a lingering argument. What happens when you want to let go, but can't? This is a perfect opportunity to look at the clinging energy. Close your eyes and ask the memory of the miscommunication to step away from your body. What are you sensing? Is there more space around your body? Play with this concept in relation to anything that lights up for you and ask it to step away from you. If it does not move, where might the attachment be in your body? If this does not work for you, just try to observe the energy and find its location. Is it behind you? Is it in front of you?

a simple reminder

By practicing this clearing meditation, we can begin to understand the dynamics of energy and how we can change its frequency and attain our most precious desires! Remember, it is just physics. Everything is energy, and you have the power to shift energy in order to create the changes you need or want to make.

"The rhythm, the dance, the choreography driven through us by any sound, may not be nothing. And it isn't nothing, it is different from nothing. It is quantum physics."

— Frederico Rochaferreira

IN CONCLUSION

Your **FIRST** and foremost task for continued emergence is to create a safe space where you can rest and focus.

SECOND: Create movement to wake up the body and aura with music that enhances the experience and flow.

THIRD: Deepen the consciousness of your body, personality, and soul connection through guided meditation and chakra clearing.

FOURTH: Learn to detach from clinging energy that is resistant to your truth.

FIFTH: Become aware of the emotional habits and story lines that invade you and affect your health!

SIXTH: Deconstruct and eliminate the "shoulds," "have tos," and "oughts" that keep you in excessive judgment.

SEVENTH: Regenerate the body/aura/mind with fresh new energy! Accept the changes, shifts, similarities, and differences in self and others.

Know that I am so grateful to share this process of emergence with you, dear reader, as we continue on this path of enlightenment—even as our physical landscape shifts with the ebb and flow of life.

We are one, as we receive the treasure of life's magical experience and witness all that is—while embracing our human connection in love and harmony.

RESOURCES

Messages from Amma: In the Language of the Heart by Amritanandamayi, and Janine Canan; Celestial Arts: Berkley, California; 2004.

Hands of Light: A Guide to Healing through the Human Energy Field: A New Paradigm for the Human Being in Health, Relationship, and Disease by Brennan, Barbara Ann; Bantam Books: New York, New York; 1993.

The Female Brain by Brizendine, Louann; Broadway Books: New York, New York; 2006.

The Male Brain by Brizendine, Louann; Bantam, 2010.

Wheels of Light: A Study of the Chakras by Bruyere, Rosalyn L; Bon Productions: New York, New York; 1989.

The Essential Enneagram: The Definitive Personality Test and Self-Discovery Guide by Daniels, David N., and Virginia Ann. Price; HarperOne; New York, New York; 2009.

Science and Health with Key to the Scriptures by Eddy, Mary Baker; First Church of Christ, Scientist; 1906.

Energy Medicine: How to Use Your Body's Energies for Optimum Health and Vitality by Eden, Donna; Jeremy P. Tarcher: Los Angeles, CA; 1999.

Psychic Psychology by Friedlander, John, and Gloria Hemsher; North Atlantic Books: Berkley, CA; 2011.

The Diamond in Your Pocket: Discovering Your True Radiance by Gangaji; Sounds True: Lousiville, Colorado; 2007.

Letting Go: The Pathway of Surrender by Hawkins, David R.; Hay House: Carlsbad, California; 2014.

Heal Your Body: The Mental Causes for Physical Illness and the Metaphysical Way to Overcome Them by Hay, Louise L; Hay House: Carlsbad, California; 2012.

The Death of the Mythic God: The Rise of Evolutionary Spirituality by Marion, Jim; Hampton Roads Pub.; Newburyport, Massachusetts; 2004.

Taking a Stand: 25 Insights to an Incredible Life by Schweppe, Matt; Balboa Press: Carlsbad, California; 2016.

The Forty Rules of Love by Shafak, Elif; Viking: London, England; 2010.

The Creative Habit: Learn It and Use It for Life by Tharp, Twyla, and Mark Reiter; Simon & Schuster: New York, New York; 2003.

The Attention Revolution: Unlocking the Power of the Focused Mind by Wallace, B. Alan; Wisdom Publications: Somerville, Massachusetts; 2010.

Inspired Action: Create More Purpose, Productivity, & Peace in Your Life by Wells, Erin Elizabeth, M.DIV.; Chosen Course LLC: Salem, Massachusetts; 2016.

Autobiography of a Yogi by Yogananda, Paramahansa; Self Realization Fellowship: Los Angeles, California; 2018.

ABOUT THE AUTHOR

As a child, Fran's world was surrounded in music, dance, singing, and believing in positive thought and philosophy. Her connection with the metaphysical world was a natural state of being. She started at the age of four dancing in a barn with a ballet barre she could never reach, but it didn't matter ~ she was hooked. There was something about expressing emotions, moving energy with her body that fit like a glove.

Fran went on to receive a BFA in dance, and for many years performed, choreographed, and taught children, and adults in private and group classes. She still performs when she gets the chance.

Her interest and training in energy healing started in 1999, with world-renowned energy healer, Rosalyn L. Bruyere, thus connecting with the metaphysical aspect of her life. Fran worked as an energy healer for the Alliance Institute for Integrative Medicine under Drs. Steve and Sandi Amoils in Cincinnati, Ohio. Subsequently, Fran began developing her meditation and psychic skills with noted psychic healers John Friedlander and Gloria Hemsher, authors of the definitive books *Basic Psychic Development* and *Psychic Psychology*.

Fran's additional work in the field includes eight years as an energy consultant for the staff at The Affinity Center for ADD Adult and Children in Cincinnati, Ohio. Fran received her certification as an accredited Enneagram teacher and trainer at The Conscious Living Center in Cincinnati, Ohio.

Combining these skills into a method of teaching has been an ongoing goal for Fran. Her passion is to integrate all of these tools to open up the conscious mind, body, and spirit. She integrates and offers her experience and skills to her clients and students through a variety of consultations in energy communication. Visit FranBailey.net for more information including consultations, classes, events, bookings, and more.

Printed in the United States
By Bookmasters